A FATHER'S HEART

A Bible Study Through Proverbs

Bruce Stapleton

MOVEMENTUM
PRESS

A Father's Heart

A Bible Study Through Proverbs

Published by Movementum Press

This book is a work of non-fiction. Unless otherwise noted, the author and the publisher make no explicit guarantees as to the accuracy of the information in this book. In some cases, the names of people and places have been altered to protect privacy.

This book is a part of the Fathering Strong Fatherhood Workshop Series of publications and may be ordered by going to www.fatheringstrongbook.com.
Other resources that accompany this book include:
Fathering Strong – God's Blueprint for Leading Your Family
Fathering Strong: Fatherhood Awakening and 30-day Devotional and Journal
Fathering Strong – A 90-day Devotional Journey
Fathering Strong Fatherhood Workshop - Participant Workbook
Fathering Strong Fatherhood Workshop - Facilitator Guide

Because of the dynamic nature of the Internet, any web addresses or links contained in this book may have changed since publication and may no longer be valid.

Scripture quotations are taken from the Holy Bible, NEW INTERNATIONAL VERSION, NIV Copyright© 1973, 1978, 1984, 2011 by Biblica, Inc.
Used by permission. All rights reserved worldwide.

Paperback

ISBN: 979-8-9985544-9-0

TABLE OF CONTENT

Welcome. You've picked up this study because you want to grow—not just as a man, but as a dad. That desire alone speaks volumes about your heart. The book of Proverbs was written largely as a father's instruction to his son, making it perhaps the most relevant book in Scripture for your role as a dad.

King Solomon, the primary author of Proverbs, understood something profound: wisdom isn't just intellectual knowledge—it's the practical skill of living life well. And as fathers, we need that skill desperately. Throughout Proverbs, Solomon addresses the core challenges every father faces—challenges that transcend culture and time. He speaks to the weight of our words and how they shape our children's souls. He wrestles with the tension between discipline and grace, showing us that true love sometimes requires correction. He calls us to model integrity in a world that often rewards compromise. He warns us about the seductive pull of foolishness and how to guard our children against it. He teaches us about the power of diligence and the dignity of honest work. And he opens our eyes to the spiritual battle for our children's hearts, reminding us that wisdom begins with fearing the Lord.

This study will walk you through six major topics that form the foundation of biblical fatherhood:

- **The Foundation of Fatherhood** (establishing the fear of the Lord as our starting point),
- **The Power of Your Words** (learning to speak life over our children),
- **Discipline and Love** (understanding how correction flows from the heart of God),
- **Teaching Integrity and Character** (modeling and instilling moral courage),
- **The Danger of Foolishness** (recognizing and redirecting our children away from destructive paths),
- **Work, Diligence, and Provision** (teaching the value of honest labor and faithful stewardship).

Each of these themes runs throughout Proverbs like golden threads, weaving together a tapestry of what it means to father well.

This study is designed to meet you where you are—whether you're a new dad holding your infant at 3 AM, a father of teenagers navigating the turbulent waters of adolescence, or a grandfather watching your legacy unfold in the next generation. The principles in Proverbs are timeless because they flow from the heart of our Heavenly Father, the perfect Dad, who models for us what fatherhood should look like.

All Scripture references in this study are taken from the New International Version (NIV). As you work through each week, I encourage you to read through the entire chapters that are highlighted in the study focus. This broader context will give you a deeper understanding of the meaning within each message and help you see how these individual verses fit into Solomon's larger teaching on wisdom and godly living.

USING THE WEEKLY STUDY WORKSHEET

To help you get the most out of this study, we've included a **Weekly Study Worksheet** that you can use alongside each chapter. This worksheet is designed to move you from simply reading about biblical fatherhood to actually living it out in your home.

The worksheet guides you through seven key areas each week:

Part 1: Personal Reflection - Before diving into the week's topic, you'll assess where you currently are as a father. What challenges are you facing? What do you hope to learn? How would you rate yourself in this week's topic area? This honest self-assessment prepares your heart to receive what God wants to teach you.

Part 2: Scripture Study - You'll write out the key verses for the week and reflect on what stands out to you. There's something powerful about writing Scripture by hand—it slows you down and helps the truth sink deeper into your heart.

Part 3: Personal Application - This is where the rubber meets the road. You'll identify specific areas where you need to grow and think through how this week's teaching applies to each of your children individually. Every child is different, and this section helps you customize your approach based on their unique ages, stages, and needs.

Part 4: Action Steps - Knowledge without action is useless. Each week, you'll commit to three specific, concrete actions you'll take. These aren't vague intentions—they're measurable steps that will move you forward as a father.

Part 5: Prayer & Accountability - You'll identify your prayer focus for the week, choose a Scripture to memorize, and note your accountability partner. Fatherhood isn't meant to be done alone. Having another man who can check in with you, encourage you, and challenge you is invaluable.

Part 6: Daily Notes - Throughout the week, you'll track what you actually did each day. This daily check-in keeps you accountable and helps you see patterns in your fathering. It's easy to have good intentions on Sunday and forget them by Wednesday. This section keeps the week's focus front and center.

Part 7: Weekly Review - At the end of each week, you'll reflect on your wins, challenges, and what God taught you. You'll also practice gratitude by identifying three things you're grateful for about your children. This weekly review helps you celebrate progress, learn from setbacks, and maintain a heart of thankfulness.

The worksheet is designed to be practical, not burdensome. It should take you 10-15 minutes at the beginning of the week to complete Parts 1-5, just a minute or two each day for Part 6, and another 10 minutes at the end of the week for Part 7. That's a small investment of time for a potentially life-changing impact on your family.

You can photocopy the worksheet for each week of the study, or download additional copies at www.fatheringstrongbook.com/resources. Some fathers find it helpful to keep all their completed worksheets in a binder as a record of their growth journey. Years from now, you'll be able to look back and see how God has worked in your life and in your children's lives.

Remember: this isn't about perfection. It's about progress. It's about being intentional. It's about showing up, day after day, and doing the hard work of fatherhood with God's help. The worksheet is simply a tool to help you do that more effectively.

So, grab a pen, find a quiet spot, and let's begin this journey together. Your children are worth it. Your family is worth it. And by God's grace, you're going to grow into the father He's called you to be.

STUDY FOCUS: PROVERBS 1:1-7

"The fear of the LORD is the beginning of knowledge, but fools despise wisdom and instruction." (Proverbs 1:7)

OPENING REFLECTION

Before we can lead our children anywhere, we must know where we're going. Before we can teach wisdom, we must pursue it ourselves. This first week establishes the foundation upon which everything else is built: the fear of the Lord.

But what does it mean to "fear" God? This isn't cowering terror—it's reverent awe. It's recognizing who God is and who we are in relation to Him. It's understanding that He is the source of all wisdom, and without Him, we're just making educated guesses about how to raise our kids.

DEEP DIVE

Read Proverbs 1:1-7 slowly. Notice that Solomon begins by stating his purpose: "for gaining wisdom and instruction; for understanding words of insight; for receiving instruction in prudent behavior, doing what is right and just and fair" (vv. 2-3). This is what we want for our children, isn't it? We want them to be wise, to understand life, to behave prudently, to do what's right.

But here's the crucial point: verse 7 tells us where all of this begins. Not with good parenting techniques. Not with the right school district. Not even with church attendance. It begins with the fear of the LORD.

As fathers, we must model this fear. Our children are watching us. They see whether we truly reverence God or just give Him lip service. They notice if we pray only at meals or if we actually walk with God throughout our day. They observe whether Scripture shapes our decisions or just decorates our coffee mugs.

PERSONAL APPLICATION

Ask yourself these questions:

1. Do my children see me pursuing God, or do they just see me taking them to church?
2. When I face a difficult decision, do I turn to God's Word first, or is it my last resort?
3. Am I modeling the fear of the Lord, or am I teaching my kids that God is just a nice addition to an already full life?

The fear of the Lord isn't something you can fake. Your kids will see through it. But here's the good news: it's also something you can grow in. Every day, you have the opportunity to demonstrate to your children what it looks like to walk with God.

1. **Start a morning routine with God.** Even if it's just ten minutes before everyone wakes up, let your children occasionally catch you reading your Bible or praying. Don't make a show of it, but don't hide it either.

2. **Speak about God naturally.** When something good happens, thank God out loud. When you face a challenge, mention that you're praying about it. Make God part of your everyday conversation, not just Sunday talk.

3. **Admit when you're wrong.** The fear of the Lord includes humility. When you mess up with your kids, apologize. Show them that even Dad needs God's grace and wisdom.

4. **Ask your children what they think about God.** Create space for spiritual conversations. Don't lecture—listen. Their honest questions and observations will show you where they are spiritually and where you need to guide them.

PRAYER FOR THIS WEEK

"My Heavenly Father, I confess that I often try to parent in my own strength and wisdom. I forget that You are the source of all wisdom, and without You, I'm lost. Teach me to fear You—not with terror, but with reverent awe. Help me to model for my children what it looks like to walk with You daily. Give me the humility to admit when I don't have the answers and the faith to trust that You do. Make me the father my children need, and make them children who fear and love You. In Jesus' name, Amen."

NOTES

A Father's Heart

Weekly Study Worksheet

Week 1   **Topic:** The Foundation of Fatherhood   **Date Started** _____

Part 1: Personal Reflection

1. What challenges am I currently facing as a father?

2. What do I hope to learn or grow in this week?

3. On a scale of 1-10, how would I rate myself in this week's topic area? _____

Part 2: Scripture Study

Key Verse(s): Write out the main verse(s) for this week's study:

What stands out to me?

Part 3: Personal Application

Where I need to grow based on this week's study:

How this applies to each child:

Child: _____ Age/Stage:_____ How this applies: _____

Child: _____ Age/Stage:_____ How this applies: _____

Child: _____ Age/Stage:_____ How this applies: _____

Part 4: Action Steps

Three specific actions I'll take this week:

1. _____

2. _____

3. _____

Part 5: Prayer & Accountability

This week's prayer focus:

Scripture to memorize:

Accountability Partner: _____. Check-in Date: _____

Part 6: Daily Notes

Day	What I Did	Results/Lessons Learned
Mon		
Tues		
Wed		
Thu		
Fri		
Sat		
Sun		

Part 7: Weekly Review

Wins this week:

Challenges this week:

What God taught me:

Three things I'm grateful for about my children:

1. _____

2. _____

3. _____

"The fear of the LORD is the beginning of knowledge, but fools despise wisdom and instruction – Proverbs 1:7

STUDY FOCUS: PROVERBS 12:18, 15:1, 16:24, 18:21

"The tongue has the power of life and death, and those who love it will eat its fruit." (Proverbs 18:21)

OPENING REFLECTION

Dad, your words carry weight. More weight than you probably realize. A single sentence from you can build up your child's confidence or tear it down. Your tone can communicate love or contempt. Your words can inspire courage or instill fear.

Proverbs has more to say about the tongue and our words than almost any other topic. Why? Because our words reveal our hearts, and they shape the hearts of those who hear them—especially our children.

DEEP DIVE

Let's look at several key verses about words:

Proverbs 12:18 - "The words of the reckless pierce like swords, but the tongue of the wise brings healing."

Think about the last time you spoke recklessly to your child. Maybe you were tired. Maybe they pushed your buttons. Maybe you were stressed about work. Whatever the reason, your words pierced like a sword. We've all been there. But the contrast here is powerful: wise words bring healing. Your words have the power to heal the wounds that life inflicts on your children.

Proverbs 15:1 - "A gentle answer turns away wrath, but a harsh word stirs up anger."

How many arguments with your kids could have been avoided if you'd responded gently instead of harshly? When your teenager talks back, your natural instinct might be to escalate. But wisdom says: respond gently. It takes strength to be gentle. It takes self-control. But it changes everything.

Proverbs 16:24 - "Gracious words are a honeycomb, sweet to the soul and healing to the bones."

When was the last time you spoke gracious words to your children? Not just "good job" or "I love you" (though those matter), but truly gracious words that spoke to their soul? Words that affirmed their character, not just their performance? Words that reminded them of their identity in Christ?

Proverbs 18:21 - "The tongue has the power of life and death, and those who love it will eat its fruit."

This is the sobering reality: your words are literally speaking life or death over your children. Not physically, but spiritually and emotionally. Every day, you're either building them up or tearing them down. You're either speaking courage into them or fear. You're either affirming their worth or questioning it.

PERSONAL APPLICATION

Let's get specific. Think about your children individually. For each child, ask yourself:

1. What words have I spoken over them recently that brought encouragement? What words brought harm?
2. Do I speak more criticism or more encouragement?
3. When I discipline, are my words aimed at correcting behavior or attacking character?
4. Do my children know, beyond any doubt, that I believe in them?

Here's a hard truth: you can't give what you don't have. If you're constantly critical of yourself, you'll be critical of your kids. If you're harsh with yourself, you'll be harsh with them. The words you speak to yourself matter too.

THE THREE TYPES OF WORDS YOUR CHILDREN NEED

1. Words of Affirmation

Your children need to hear that you love them, that you're proud of them, that they matter. Not just when they perform well, but simply because they're yours. "I love you." "I'm proud of you." "I'm so glad you're my son/daughter." These simple phrases are like water to a thirsty soul.

2. Words of Instruction

Proverbs is full of a father instructing his son. Your children need your wisdom. They need you to teach them about life, about God, about character. But instruction without relationship leads to rebellion. Make sure your words of affirmation outnumber your words of instruction.

3. Words of Correction

Yes, you need to correct your children. But correction should be specific, focused on behavior not character, and always wrapped in love. "That choice was foolish" is very different from "You're foolish." One corrects behavior; the other attacks identity.

PRACTICAL STEPS THIS WEEK

1. **The 5:1 Ratio.** Research suggests that relationships thrive when there are five positive interactions for every negative one. This week, aim for a 5:1 ratio with each of your children. Five encouraging, affirming, or positive words for every corrective or critical word.
2. **Write a letter.** Write each of your children a letter telling them what you see in them, what you love about them, what you're proud of. Be specific. Keep it. Give it to them at the right time—maybe this week, maybe years from now.
3. **Apologize for harsh words.** If you've spoken harshly to your children recently, apologize. Don't justify it. Don't explain it away. Just say, "I was wrong. My words were harsh. Will you forgive me?" This models humility and shows them that even Dad needs grace.
4. **Pray before you speak.** When you feel anger rising, when you're about to correct or discipline, take a breath and pray silently: "Lord, give me Your words." It only takes a second, but it can change everything.

5. **Speak life at bedtime.** Make it a habit to speak words of life over your children before they go to sleep. Even if the day was hard, even if there was conflict, end the day with words that affirm their worth and your love.

PRAYER FOR THIS WEEK

"Lord, set a guard over my mouth. Help me to speak words that bring life, not death. Forgive me for the times I've spoken harshly, critically, or carelessly to my children. Give me wisdom to know when to speak and when to be silent. Fill my heart with Your love so that my words overflow with grace. Help me to build up my children with my words, to speak courage into their fears, and to affirm their identity in You. Make my tongue an instrument of healing, not harm. In Jesus' name, Amen."

NOTES

A Father's Heart

Weekly Study Worksheet

Week 2   **Topic:** The Power of Your Words   **Date Started** _____

Part 1: Personal Reflection

1. What challenges am I currently facing as a father?

2. What do I hope to learn or grow in this week?

3. On a scale of 1-10, how would I rate myself in this week's topic area? _____

Part 2: Scripture Study

Key Verse(s): Write out the main verse(s) for this week's study:

What stands out to me?

Part 3: Personal Application

Where I need to grow based on this week's study:

How this applies to each child:

Child: _____ Age/Stage:_____ How this applies: _____

Child: _____ Age/Stage:_____ How this applies: _____

Child: _____ Age/Stage:_____ How this applies: _____

Part 4: Action Steps

Three specific actions I'll take this week:

1. _____

2. _____

3. _____

Part 5: Prayer & Accountability

This week's prayer focus:

Scripture to memorize:

Accountability Partner: _____. Check-in Date: _____

Part 6: Daily Notes

Day	What I Did	Results/Lessons Learned
Mon		
Tues		
Wed		
Thu		
Fri		
Sat		
Sun		

Part 7: Weekly Review

Wins this week:

Challenges this week:

What God taught me:

Three things I'm grateful for about my children:

1. _____

2. _____

3. _____

"The fear of the LORD is the beginning of knowledge, but fools despise wisdom and instruction − Proverbs 1:7

"Whoever spares the rod hates their children, but the one who loves their children is careful to discipline them." (Proverbs 13:24)

OPENING REFLECTION

This is perhaps the most challenging aspect of fatherhood: discipline. We live in a culture that's confused about discipline, swinging between permissiveness and harshness. But Proverbs offers us a different path— one that holds discipline and love together in perfect tension.

Before we dive in, let's be clear: discipline is not abuse. Discipline is not anger unleashed. Discipline is not about control or domination. Biblical discipline is always motivated by love and aimed at the child's good.

DEEP DIVE

Proverbs 3:11-12 - "My son, do not despise the LORD's discipline, and do not resent his rebuke, because the LORD disciplines those he loves, as a father the son he delights in."

This is the foundation for all discipline: God disciplines those He loves. Think about that. God's discipline isn't evidence of His anger toward us—it's evidence of His love. He cares too much about us to let us continue in destructive patterns. He loves us too much to leave us as we are.

This is the model for our discipline. We discipline our children not because we're angry (though we might feel angry), but because we love them. We care too much about their character to let them continue in foolishness. We love them too much to let them grow up without boundaries.

Notice also that God disciplines "the son he delights in." Discipline and delight go together. You can discipline your children while still delighting in them. In fact, you must. If your children only experience your correction and never your delight, they'll grow up believing they can never please you.

Proverbs 13:24 - "Whoever spares the rod hates their children, but the one who loves their children is careful to discipline them."

This is a hard verse for modern ears. But let's understand what it's really saying. The "rod" in ancient Israel was a shepherd's tool—used to guide, protect, and correct the sheep. It wasn't primarily a weapon; it was a tool of care.

The point isn't the specific method of discipline (though physical discipline, when done appropriately, isn't ruled out). The point is that failing to discipline your children is actually a form of hatred. That sounds harsh, but think about it: if you let your child continue in foolishness, if you never correct them, if you never set boundaries, you're setting them up for a life of pain and failure. That's not love—that's neglect.

True love is "careful to discipline." Notice that word: careful. Discipline should never be reckless, never done in anger, never excessive. It should be thoughtful, measured, and always aimed at the child's good.

Proverbs 19:18 - "Discipline your children, for in that there is hope; do not be a willing party to their death."

Discipline gives your children hope. Without discipline, without boundaries, without correction, children grow up without the character they need to navigate life successfully. They become adults who can't handle authority, can't delay gratification, can't control their impulses. That's a kind of death—not physical, but spiritual and emotional.

Proverbs 22:6 - "Start children off on the way they should go, and even when they are old they will not turn from it."

This is both a promise and a responsibility. You're not just managing your children's behavior today—you're shaping who they'll become tomorrow. The habits, values, and character you instill now will stay with them for life.

But notice: "the way they should go." Not the way you want them to go. Not the way that makes you look good. Not the way that fulfills your unfulfilled dreams. The way they should go—according to how God made them, according to God's purposes for their lives.

Proverbs 23:13-14 - "Do not withhold discipline from a child; if you punish them with the rod, they will not die. Punish them with the rod and save them from death."

Again, the emphasis is on not withholding discipline. Your children need correction. They need boundaries. They need to learn that actions have consequences. If they don't learn this from you, in the safety of your love, they'll learn it from the world, which is far less merciful.

Proverbs 29:15 - "A rod and a reprimand impart wisdom, but a child left undisciplined disgraces its mother."

Notice that both correction ("rod") and instruction ("reprimand") are needed. Discipline without explanation is just punishment. Your children need to understand why they're being disciplined, what they did wrong, and what they should do instead.

THE PURPOSE OF DISCIPLINE

Discipline has several purposes:

1. To Teach Wisdom
Discipline is fundamentally educational. You're teaching your children how to live wisely. Every act of discipline is a lesson: this behavior leads to pain; that behavior leads to blessing.

2. To Build Character
Discipline shapes character. It teaches self-control, respect for authority, delayed gratification, and responsibility. These are the building blocks of a successful life.

3. To Protect
Sometimes discipline protects children from immediate danger (don't touch the stove, don't run into the street). Sometimes it protects them from long-term consequences (lying will destroy your relationships, laziness will ruin your future).

4. To Reflect God's Character

When you discipline your children lovingly and consistently, you're giving them a picture of how God relates to His children. You're teaching them that God is both loving and just, both merciful and holy.

THE PRACTICE OF DISCIPLINE

Here are some principles for biblical discipline:

1. Discipline in Love, Not Anger

If you're angry, take a break. Tell your child, "What you did was wrong, and we're going to address it. But I need a few minutes first." Then go pray, calm down, and come back ready to discipline in love.

2. Be Consistent

Inconsistent discipline is confusing and ineffective. If something is wrong today, it's wrong tomorrow. If there's a consequence for a behavior, enforce it every time.

3. Make the Punishment Fit the Crime

Don't overreact. A minor infraction doesn't deserve a major punishment. And don't punish in a way that's unrelated to the offense. Natural consequences are often the best teachers.

4. Always Explain

Your children need to understand why they're being disciplined. Explain what they did wrong, why it was wrong, and what they should do instead. This turns discipline into discipleship.

5. Affirm Your Love

Before and after discipline, affirm your love. "I love you, and that's why I can't let you continue in this behavior." "I love you, and nothing you do will ever change that."

6. Point to the Gospel

Use discipline as an opportunity to point your children to Jesus. "We all sin. We all need forgiveness. That's why Jesus died for us—to pay the price for our sin and to give us the power to change."

PERSONAL APPLICATION

1. How would you describe your approach to discipline? Are you too harsh? Too lenient? Inconsistent?
2. Do your children understand that you discipline them because you love them?
3. Are you disciplining in anger or in love?
4. Do you explain why you're disciplining, or do you just punish?
5. Are you consistent, or do your children never know what to expect?

PRACTICAL STEPS THIS WEEK

1. **Establish clear expectations.** Sit down with your children and clearly communicate your expectations and the consequences for not meeting them. This eliminates confusion and makes discipline more effective.
2. **Create a discipline plan.** Before you're in the heat of the moment, decide how you'll handle common infractions. This helps you be consistent and prevents you from overreacting.

3. **Practice the pause.** When your child does something that requires discipline, pause before responding. Take a breath. Pray. Then respond calmly and lovingly.
4. **Follow up after discipline.** After you've disciplined your child, follow up later. Ask if they understand why they were disciplined. Affirm your love. Pray with them.
5. **Evaluate your discipline.** At the end of each week, reflect on how you disciplined. Were you consistent? Loving? Fair? What do you need to change?

PRAYER FOR THIS WEEK

"Father, give me wisdom to discipline my children well. Help me to discipline in love, not anger. Give me consistency, patience, and self-control. Help me to see discipline not as a burden but as an opportunity to shape my children's character and point them to You. Forgive me for the times I've been too harsh or too lenient. Give me discernment to know when to correct and when to show mercy. Help my children to see Your love through my discipline. In Jesus' name, Amen."

NOTES

A Father's Heart

Weekly Study Worksheet

Week 3   Topic: Discipline and Love   **Date Started** _____

Part 1: Personal Reflection

1. What challenges am I currently facing as a father?

2. What do I hope to learn or grow in this week?

3. On a scale of 1-10, how would I rate myself in this week's topic area? _____

Part 2: Scripture Study

Key Verse(s): Write out the main verse(s) for this week's study:

What stands out to me?

Part 3: Personal Application

Where I need to grow based on this week's study:

How this applies to each child:

Child: _____ Age/Stage:_____ How this applies: _____

Child: _____ Age/Stage:_____ How this applies: _____

Child: _____ Age/Stage:_____ How this applies: _____

Part 4: Action Steps

Three specific actions I'll take this week:

1._____

2._____

3._____

Part 5: Prayer & Accountability

This week's prayer focus:

Scripture to memorize:

Accountability Partner: _____. Check-in Date: _____

Part 6: Daily Notes

Day	What I Did	Results/Lessons Learned
Mon		
Tues		
Wed		
Thu		
Fri		
Sat		
Sun		

Part 7: Weekly Review

Wins this week:

Challenges this week:

What God taught me:

Three things I'm grateful for about my children:

1. _____

2. _____

3. _____

"The fear of the LORD is the beginning of knowledge, but fools despise wisdom and instruction – Proverbs 1:7

STUDY FOCUS: PROVERBS 10:9, 11:3, 12:22, 20:7, 28:6

"The integrity of the upright guides them, but the unfaithful are destroyed by their duplicity." (Proverbs 11:3)

OPENING REFLECTION

Dad, you're not just raising children—you're raising future adults. And the character they develop now will determine the kind of adults they become. Will they be people of integrity or people who compromise? Will they be honest or deceptive? Will they do what's right even when it's hard, or will they take the easy way out?

The answer to these questions depends largely on what you model and what you teach. Your children are watching you. They see whether you keep your promises. They notice how your treat others or lie to get out of commitments. They observe whether you do what's right when no one's watching.

DEEP DIVE

Proverbs 10:9 - "Whoever walks in integrity walks securely, but whoever takes crooked paths will be found out."

Integrity provides security. When you live with integrity, you don't have to worry about being found out. You don't have to remember what lies you told to whom. You don't have to look over your shoulder. There's a freedom and peace that comes with integrity.

But the opposite is also true: those who take crooked paths will be found out. Maybe not today, maybe not tomorrow, but eventually. Sin has a way of coming to light. And when it does, the consequences are devastating.

As fathers, we need to teach our children this truth. Integrity isn't just about being good—it's about being wise. It's about building a life on a solid foundation rather than on shifting sand.

Proverbs 11:3 - "The integrity of the upright guides them, but the unfaithful are destroyed by their duplicity."

Integrity is like an internal compass. When you have integrity, you always know which way to go. You don't have to wonder what's right—your character guides you. But duplicity—living a double life, saying one thing and doing another—is destructive. It destroys relationships, reputations, and ultimately, the person themselves.

Our children need to see that integrity isn't just a nice idea—it's essential for a good life. And they need to see it modeled in us.

Proverbs 12:22 - "The LORD detests lying lips, but he delights in people who are trustworthy."

This is strong language. God doesn't just dislike lying—He detests it. Why? Because lying is the opposite of His character. God is truth. When we lie, we're acting contrary to the very nature of God.

But notice the contrast: God delights in people who are trustworthy. He takes pleasure in those who tell the truth, keep their promises, and live with integrity. This is the kind of person we want our children to become.

Proverbs 20:7 - "The righteous lead blameless lives; blessed are their children after them."

This is both encouraging and sobering. When you live with integrity, your children are blessed. They benefit from your good reputation. They learn from your example. They inherit a legacy of righteousness.

But the opposite is also true. When you compromise, when you cut corners, when you live without integrity, your children suffer. They learn that character doesn't really matter. They inherit a legacy of compromise.

Proverbs 28:6 - "Better the poor whose walk is blameless than the rich whose ways are perverse."

In our culture, we often measure success by wealth, status, and achievement. But God measures success by character. He'd rather you be poor with integrity than rich with compromise.

This is a crucial lesson for our children. In a world that tells them to get ahead at any cost, we need to teach them that character matters more than success. That who they are is more important than what they achieve. That integrity is worth more than any amount of money or status.

THE COMPONENTS OF CHARACTER

What does it mean to have character? Let's break it down:

1. Honesty
This is the foundation. Character begins with telling the truth—even when it's hard, even when it costs you, even when a lie would be easier. Teach your children that honesty isn't just about not lying—it's about being truthful in all things.

2. Integrity
Integrity means your private life matches your public life. You're the same person when no one's watching as you are when everyone's watching. You do what's right not because someone might see, but because it's right.

3. Responsibility
Character means taking responsibility for your actions. It means not making excuses, not blaming others, not playing the victim. It means owning your mistakes and making them right.

4. Faithfulness
Character means keeping your commitments. When you say you'll do something, you do it. When you make a promise, you keep it. Your word is your bond.

5. Courage
Character requires courage—the courage to do what's right even when it's unpopular, even when it costs you, even when you're afraid. Courage isn't the absence of fear; it's doing what's right despite the fear.

TEACHING CHARACTER TO YOUR CHILDREN

How do you teach character? Here are some practical ways:

1. Model It

This is the most important. Your children will become what they see, not what you say. If you want them to have integrity, you must have integrity. If you want them to be honest, you must be honest. If you want them to be responsible, you must be responsible.

2. Talk About It

Don't assume your children will just pick up character by osmosis. Talk about it explicitly. When you see examples of good character (in real life, in books, in movies), point it out. When you see examples of poor character, use them as teaching moments.

3. Praise It

When your children demonstrate good character, praise them. Not just when they succeed, but when they show integrity, honesty, courage, or responsibility. "I'm proud of you for telling the truth even though you knew you'd get in trouble." "I noticed how you kept your commitment even when you didn't feel like it. That's character."

4. Correct the Lack of It

When your children lie, cheat, or compromise, address it immediately. Don't let it slide. Explain why it's wrong and what the consequences are. But also explain how they can do better next time.

5. Create Opportunities for It

Give your children opportunities to develop character. Give them responsibilities and hold them accountable. Put them in situations where they have to make hard choices. Let them experience the natural consequences of their choices.

PERSONAL APPLICATION

Let's get personal. Ask yourself:

1. Am I modeling integrity for my children? Are there areas where I'm compromising?
2. Do I keep my promises to my children, or do I make commitments I don't keep?
3. Am I honest in all things, or do I tell "little white lies" that teach my children that honesty is optional?
4. Do I take responsibility for my mistakes, or do I make excuses and blame others?
5. Am I the same person in private as I am in public?

These are hard questions. But they're necessary. Because your children are watching, and they're learning from what they see.

PRACTICAL STEPS THIS WEEK

1. **Identify one area where you need to grow in integrity.** Maybe it's keeping your promises. Maybe it's being honest in all things. Maybe it's taking responsibility instead of making excuses. Choose one area and commit to growing in it this week.

2. **Have a conversation with your children about character.** Ask them what they think character means. Ask them who they know who has good character and why. Use this as an opportunity to teach.
3. **Catch your children demonstrating good character and praise them.** Look for opportunities to affirm character, not just achievement.
4. **Read a biography together.** Choose someone known for their character (like Abraham Lincoln, Marin Luther King Jr. or Mother Theresa) and read about their life together. Talk about the choices they made and why.
5. **Create a family motto or values statement.** Sit down as a family and decide what values are most important to you. Write them down and post them somewhere visible. Refer to them regularly.

PRAYER FOR THIS WEEK

"Lord, make me a man of integrity. Help me to be the same person in private as I am in public. Give me the courage to do what's right even when it's hard. Help me to model integrity for my children so that they learn to value character above success. Forgive me for the times I've compromised, and give me the strength to live blamelessly. Help my children to become people of integrity who walk securely because they walk in truth. In Jesus' name, Amen."

NOTES

A Father's Heart

Weekly Study Worksheet

Week 4 Topic: Teaching Integrity and Character   **Date Started** _____

Part 1: Personal Reflection

1. What challenges am I currently facing as a father?

2. What do I hope to learn or grow in this week?

3. On a scale of 1-10, how would I rate myself in this week's topic area? _____

Part 2: Scripture Study

Key Verse(s): Write out the main verse(s) for this week's study:

What stands out to me?

Part 3: Personal Application

Where I need to grow based on this week's study:

How this applies to each child:

Child: _____ Age/Stage:_____ How this applies: _____

Child: _____ Age/Stage:_____ How this applies: _____

Child: _____ Age/Stage:_____ How this applies: _____

Part 4: Action Steps

Three specific actions I'll take this week:

1. _____

2. _____

3. _____

Part 5: Prayer & Accountability

This week's prayer focus:

Scripture to memorize:

Accountability Partner: _____. Check-in Date: _____

Part 6: Daily Notes

Day	What I Did	Results/Lessons Learned
Mon		
Tues		
Wed		
Thu		
Fri		
Sat		
Sun		

Part 7: Weekly Review

Wins this week:

Challenges this week:

What God taught me:

Three things I'm grateful for about my children:

1. _____

2. _____

3. _____

"The fear of the LORD is the beginning of knowledge, but fools despise wisdom and instruction – Proverbs 1:7

STUDY FOCUS: PROVERBS 1:7, 10:23, 12:15, 14:16, 17:10, 26:11

"Fools find pleasure in wicked schemes, but a person of understanding delights in wisdom." (Proverbs 10:23)

OPENING REFLECTION

Proverbs talks a lot about fools. Not because God wants to insult anyone, but because foolishness is dangerous. It's destructive. As fathers, we need to help our children recognize foolishness—in themselves and in others—so they can avoid it.

But here's the thing: we're all foolish sometimes. We all make foolish choices. The question is: will we learn from our foolishness, or will we persist in it? Will we grow in wisdom, or will we remain fools?

DEEP DIVE

Proverbs 1:7 - "The fear of the LORD is the beginning of knowledge, but fools despise wisdom and instruction."

We started with this verse in Week 1, but it's worth revisiting. The defining characteristic of a fool is that they despise wisdom and instruction. They don't want to learn. They don't want to be corrected. They think they know better.

We need to cultivate in our children a love for wisdom and a willingness to receive instruction. We need to teach them that being teachable is a strength, not a weakness. Admitting you don't know something is wise, not foolish.

Proverbs 10:23 - "Fools find pleasure in wicked schemes, but a person of understanding delights in wisdom."

Fools are attracted to what's wrong. They find pleasure in things that are destructive. They're drawn to sin like moths to a flame. But people of understanding—wise people—delight in wisdom. They're attracted to what's good and right and true.

Our children are constantly being pulled in different directions. The world is offering them all kinds of foolish pleasures. As fathers, we need to help them develop a taste for wisdom, to find delight in what's good.

Proverbs 12:15 - "The way of fools seems right to them, but the wise listen to advice."

This is one of the most dangerous aspects of foolishness: fools don't know they're fools. They think they're right. They're confident in their foolishness. That's why they don't listen to advice—they don't think they need it.

Wise people, on the other hand, know they don't have all the answers. They seek advice. They listen to counsel. They're humble enough to admit when they're wrong.

It is important to teach our children to listen to advice—especially from those who are older and wiser. We need to help them develop humility and teachability.

Proverbs 14:16 - "The wise fear the LORD and shun evil, but a fool is hotheaded and yet feels secure."

Fools are characterized by two things: they're hotheaded (they act impulsively, without thinking), and they feel secure (they're overconfident, they don't see the danger). This is a deadly combination.

Wise people, on the other hand, fear the Lord (they have a healthy respect for God and His ways) and shun evil (they actively avoid what's wrong). They're cautious, thoughtful, and humble.

Proverbs 17:10 - "A rebuke impresses a discerning person more than a hundred lashes a fool."

This is sobering. A wise person can be corrected with a word. A fool requires a hundred lashes and still doesn't learn. Why? Because fools are unteachable. They don't want to change. They resist correction.

We need to teach our children to receive correction well. When they're corrected, do they get defensive? Do they make excuses? Or do they listen, learn, and change?

Proverbs 26:11 - "As a dog returns to its vomit, so fools repeat their folly."

This is a graphic image, but it makes the point. Fools keep making the same mistakes over and over. They don't learn from their experiences. They repeat their folly.

Wise people, on the other hand, learn from their mistakes. They don't keep doing the same foolish things expecting different results.

TYPES OF FOOLS IN PROVERBS

Proverbs actually describes several different types of fools:

1. The Simple Fool (Hebrew: "pethi")
This is someone who's naive, gullible, easily led astray. They lack experience and judgment. The good news is that simple fools can become wise if they're willing to learn. Many of our children start here—they're simple because they're young and inexperienced. Our job is to teach them wisdom so they don't stay simple.

2. The Stubborn Fool (Hebrew: "kesil")
This is someone who's closed-minded, resistant to instruction, stubborn. They think they know better. They don't want to learn. This is more serious than being simple, because stubborn fools actively resist wisdom.

3. The Hardened Fool (Hebrew: "nabal")
This is someone who's morally corrupt, who despises God and His ways. They're not just foolish—they're wicked. They've hardened their hearts against wisdom and righteousness.

4. The Mocker (Hebrew: "letz")
This is someone who ridicules wisdom, who mocks what's good and right. They're arrogant, cynical, and destructive. They don't just reject wisdom—they attack it.

We need to help our children avoid progressing through these stages of foolishness by catching foolishness early and correcting it before it hardens into something worse.

WARNING SIGNS OF FOOLISHNESS

How do you know if your child is heading down the path of foolishness? Here are some warning signs:

1. **They resist correction.** When you try to correct them, they get defensive, make excuses, or blame others.
2. **They don't learn from their mistakes.** They keep making the same foolish choices over and over.
3. **They're attracted to the wrong crowd.** They're drawn to friends who are a bad influence.
4. **They mock what's good.** They ridicule faith, virtue, wisdom, or authority.
5. **They're impulsive.** They act without thinking, without considering the consequences.
6. **They're overconfident.** They think they know better than everyone else, including you.

If you see these warning signs, don't panic. But don't ignore them either. Address them directly, lovingly, and consistently.

TEACHING YOUR CHILDREN TO AVOID FOOLISHNESS

1. Teach them to fear the Lord. This is the foundation. When children fear the Lord, they have a framework for wisdom. They understand that there's a right and wrong, and that God cares about how they live.

2. Teach them to be teachable. Praise them when they receive correction well. Model teachability yourself. Show them that being willing to learn is a strength.

3. Teach them to think before they act. Help them develop the habit of pausing before making decisions. Ask them: "What are the possible consequences of this choice? What would wisdom say?"

4. Teach them to choose their friends wisely. Proverbs says a lot about the company we keep. Help your children understand that their friends will influence them—for good or for bad.

5. Teach them to learn from their mistakes. When they make a foolish choice, don't just punish them. Help them understand what went wrong and how they can do better next time.

PERSONAL APPLICATION

1. Are there areas where you're being foolish? Are you resistant to correction? Are you repeating the same mistakes?
2. How do you respond when your children correct you or point out your mistakes? Do you model teachability?
3. Are you helping your children develop wisdom, or are you just trying to control their behavior?
4. Do your children see you seeking advice and listening to counsel, or do they see you thinking you have all the answers?

PRACTICAL STEPS THIS WEEK

1. **Have a conversation about foolishness.** Talk with your children about what foolishness is and why it's dangerous. Use examples from Proverbs or from real life.

2. **Identify one area where each of your children is being foolish.** Maybe they're not learning from their mistakes. Maybe they're resistant to correction. Maybe they're choosing the wrong friends. Address it lovingly but directly.
3. **Model teachability.** This week, intentionally seek advice about something. Let your children see you listening to counsel and being willing to change your mind.
4. **Praise teachability.** When your children receive correction well, praise them. "I'm proud of how you listened to what I said and didn't get defensive. That's wisdom."
5. **Read Proverbs together.** Choose a few verses about fools and wise people and read them together. Talk about what they mean and how they apply to your lives.

PRAYER FOR THIS WEEK

"Lord, protect my children from foolishness. Give them hearts that are teachable, minds that are open to wisdom, and spirits that fear You. Help them to learn from their mistakes and to grow in wisdom. Give me wisdom to know how to guide them, when to correct them, and how to model teachability myself. Don't let my children become fools who despise wisdom and instruction. Instead, make them people of understanding who delight in wisdom. In Jesus' name, Amen."

NOTES

A Father's Heart

Weekly Study Worksheet

Week 5 Topic: The Danger of Foolishness **Date Started** _____

Part 1: Personal Reflection

1. What challenges am I currently facing as a father?

2. What do I hope to learn or grow in this week?

3. On a scale of 1-10, how would I rate myself in this week's topic area? _____

Part 2: Scripture Study

Key Verse(s): Write out the main verse(s) for this week's study:

What stands out to me?

Part 3: Personal Application

Where I need to grow based on this week's study:

How this applies to each child:

Child: _____ Age/Stage:_____ How this applies: _____

Child: _____ Age/Stage:_____ How this applies: _____

Child: _____ Age/Stage:_____ How this applies: _____

Part 4: Action Steps

Three specific actions I'll take this week:

1._____

2._____

3._____

Part 5: Prayer & Accountability

This week's prayer focus:

Scripture to memorize:

Accountability Partner: _____. Check-in Date: _____

Part 6: Daily Notes

Day	What I Did	Results/Lessons Learned
Mon		
Tues		
Wed		
Thu		
Fri		
Sat		
Sun		

Part 7: Weekly Review

Wins this week:

Challenges this week:

What God taught me:

Three things I'm grateful for about my children:

1. _____

2. _____

3. _____

"The fear of the LORD is the beginning of knowledge, but fools despise wisdom and instruction – Proverbs 1:7

STUDY FOCUS: PROVERBS 6:6-11, 10:4-5, 12:24, 13:4, 14:23, 21:25, 24:30-34

"Go to the ant, you sluggard; consider its ways and be wise!" (Proverbs 6:6)

OPENING REFLECTION

Dad, one of the most important things you can teach your children is how to work. Not just how to do a job, but how to work with diligence, excellence, and purpose. In a culture that increasingly values comfort over character and ease over effort, teaching your children to work hard is countercultural—and essential.

Work isn't a curse—it's a gift. God worked in creation, and He made us in His image to be workers too. Work gives us purpose, dignity, and the opportunity to serve others and glorify God. But our culture has lost this understanding. Many people see work as something to be avoided or minimized. As fathers, we need to recapture a biblical vision of work and pass it on to our children.

DEEP DIVE

Proverbs 6:6-11 - "Go to the ant, you sluggard; consider its ways and be wise! It has no commander, no overseer or ruler, yet it stores its provisions in summer and gathers its food at harvest. How long will you lie there, you sluggard? When will you get up from your sleep? A little sleep, a little slumber, a little folding of the hands to rest—and poverty will come on you like a thief and scarcity like an armed man."

This is one of the most vivid passages in Proverbs about work and laziness. God tells the lazy person to learn from an ant. An ant doesn't need someone standing over it, telling it what to do. It works diligently on its own initiative. It plans ahead. It works hard when work needs to be done.

The lazy person, on the other hand, is always looking for an excuse to rest. "A little sleep, a little slumber, a little folding of the hands to rest." It's never a lot—just a little. But those "littles" add up, and before you know it, poverty has come "like a thief."

As fathers, we need to teach our children to be like the ant—to work diligently without needing constant supervision, to plan ahead, to work hard when work needs to be done.

Proverbs 10:4-5 - "Lazy hands make for poverty, but diligent hands bring wealth. He who gathers crops in summer is a prudent son, but he who sleeps during harvest is a disgraceful son."

There's a direct connection between diligence and prosperity, between laziness and poverty. This doesn't mean that everyone who works hard will be rich, or that everyone who's poor is lazy. But generally speaking, diligence leads to blessing and laziness leads to lack.

Notice the contrast in verse 5: the prudent son works when work needs to be done. The disgraceful son sleeps during harvest. Timing matters. There's a time to work and a time to rest, and wisdom knows the difference.

Proverbs 12:24 - "Diligent hands will rule, but laziness ends in forced labor."

Diligence leads to leadership and freedom. Laziness leads to servitude. When you work hard and develop skills, you create opportunities for yourself. You become valuable. You gain influence. But when you're lazy, you limit your options. You become dependent on others. You end up in positions where you have no choice but to do what you're told.

Proverbs 13:4 - "A sluggard's appetite is never filled, but the desires of the diligent are fully satisfied."

Lazy people want things, but they're not willing to work for them. They have desires, but they're never satisfied because they're not willing to put in the effort required to achieve their goals. Diligent people, on the other hand, see their desires fulfilled because they're willing to work for them.

Proverbs 14:23 - "All hard work brings a profit, but mere talk leads only to poverty."

It's easy to talk about what you're going to do. It's easy to make plans and dream dreams. But talk without work leads to poverty. It's the actual work—the hard work—that brings profit.

As fathers, we need to teach our children not just to talk about what they're going to do, but to actually do it. To follow through. To put in the work.

Proverbs 21:25 - "The craving of a sluggard will be the death of him, because his hands refuse to work."

This is a sobering verse. Laziness isn't just inconvenient—it's deadly. Not necessarily physically (though it can be), but spiritually and emotionally. Lazy people are never satisfied. They're always wanting, always craving, but never willing to work for what they want. And that unfulfilled craving eats away at them.

Proverbs 24:30-34 - "I went past the field of a sluggard, past the vineyard of someone who has no sense; thorns had come up everywhere, the ground was covered with weeds, and the stone wall was in ruins. I applied my heart to what I observed and learned a lesson from what I saw: A little sleep, a little slumber, a little folding of the hands to rest—and poverty will come on you like a thief and scarcity like an armed man."

This is a picture of what happens when you neglect your responsibilities. The field is overgrown with thorns and weeds. The wall is in ruins. Everything is falling apart. Why? Because the owner was lazy. He didn't do the work that needed to be done.

And notice: it doesn't happen all at once. It's gradual. "A little sleep, a little slumber." But eventually, the neglect catches up with you, and poverty comes "like a thief."

THE BIBLICAL VIEW OF WORK

Before we can teach our children to work, we need to understand what the Bible says about work:

1. Work is good.
God worked in creation, and He called it good. Work isn't a result of the fall—it's part of God's original design for humanity. We were made to work.

2. Work has dignity.
All honest work has dignity, whether it's manual labor or intellectual work, whether it's highly paid or low-paid. There's no hierarchy of value in God's eyes. The janitor who works diligently is just as valuable as the CEO.

3. Work is worship.

When we work with excellence and integrity, we're worshiping God. Colossians 3:23 says, "Whatever you do, work at it with all your heart, as working for the Lord, not for human masters."

4. Work serves others.

Work isn't just about making money or achieving success. It's about serving others and contributing to the common good. When you work, you're using your God-given talents and abilities to meet needs, solve problems, and make the world a better place. Your work matters because it serves people.

TEACHING YOUR CHILDREN TO WORK

So how do we instill a strong work ethic in our children? Here are some practical ways:

1. Give them age-appropriate responsibilities.

Start early. Even young children can help with simple tasks. As they grow, increase their responsibilities. Don't do everything for them—let them contribute to the household.

2. Let them experience the consequences of laziness.

If they don't do their chores, they don't get their allowance. If they don't study, they get poor grades. Natural consequences are powerful teachers.

3. Model diligence yourself.

Your children are watching how you approach your work. Do you complain constantly? Do you cut corners? Or do you work with excellence and a good attitude?

4. Celebrate hard work, not just results.

Praise the effort, not just the outcome. "I'm proud of how hard you worked on that project" is better than "I'm proud you got an A."

5. Teach them to finish what they start.

Don't let them quit when things get hard. Help them push through challenges and complete their commitments.

6. Connect work to purpose.

Help them see that work isn't just about earning money—it's about using their gifts to serve God and others.

PERSONAL APPLICATION

1. What kind of work ethic am I modeling for my children? Do they see me working diligently, or do they see me cutting corners and complaining?
2. Have I given my children age-appropriate responsibilities, or am I doing everything for them?
3. Am I teaching my children that all honest work has dignity, or am I communicating that some jobs are beneath them?
4. Do my children understand that work is worship, or do they see it as just a means to an end?

PRACTICAL STEPS THIS WEEK

1. **Assign new responsibilities.** Give each child a new chore or responsibility this week. Make sure it's age-appropriate and clearly explained.

2. **Work alongside your children.** Choose a project you can do together—yard work, cleaning the garage, fixing something. Use the time to talk about the value of work.

3. **Share your work stories.** Tell your children about your workday. Share both the challenges and the rewards. Help them see how your work serves others.

4. **Read Proverbs 6:6-11 together.** Discuss what it means and how it applies to your family.

PRAYER FOR THIS WEEK

"Lord, thank You for the gift of work. Help me to model diligence and excellence for my children. Give them a strong work ethic and help them see their work as worship. Protect them from laziness and entitlement. May they learn to work hard, serve others, and glorify You in all they do. In Jesus' name, Amen."

NOTES

A Father's Heart

Weekly Study Worksheet

Week 6 **Topic:** Work, Diligence, and Laziness **Date Started** _____

Part 1: Personal Reflection

1. What challenges am I currently facing as a father?

2. What do I hope to learn or grow in this week?

3. On a scale of 1-10, how would I rate myself in this week's topic area? _____

Part 2: Scripture Study

Key Verse(s): Write out the main verse(s) for this week's study:

What stands out to me?

Part 3: Personal Application

Where I need to grow based on this week's study:

How this applies to each child:

Child: _____ Age/Stage:_____ How this applies: _____

Child: _____ Age/Stage:_____ How this applies: _____

Child: _____ Age/Stage:_____ How this applies: _____

Part 4: Action Steps

Three specific actions I'll take this week:

1. _____

2. _____

3. _____

Part 5: Prayer & Accountability

This week's prayer focus:

Scripture to memorize:

Accountability Partner: _____. Check-in Date: _____

Part 6: Daily Notes

Day	What I Did	Results/Lessons Learned
Mon		
Tues		
Wed		
Thu		
Fri		
Sat		
Sun		

Part 7: Weekly Review

Wins this week:

Challenges this week:

What God taught me:

Three things I'm grateful for about my children:

1. _____

2. _____

3. _____

"The fear of the LORD is the beginning of knowledge, but fools despise wisdom and instruction – Proverbs 1:7

CONCLUSION: THE LEGACY YOU'RE BUILDING

Congratulations, you've completed six weeks of studying what Proverbs teaches about fatherhood. But this isn't really an ending—it's a beginning. The real work starts now, as you take what you've learned and apply it day by day, moment by moment, in the trenches of everyday life.

Let's review what we've covered:

Week 1: The Foundation of Wisdom - We learned that the fear of the Lord is the beginning of wisdom, and that our primary job as fathers is to point our children to God.

Week 2: The Power of Words - We discovered that our words have the power to build up or tear down, and that we must be intentional about speaking life to our children.

Week 3: Discipline and Love - We explored the difficult but necessary work of discipline, understanding that true love requires correction and boundaries.

Week 4: Teaching Integrity and Character - We examined the importance of modeling and teaching integrity, recognizing that our children are watching and learning from everything we do.

Week 5: The Danger of Foolishness - We identified the warning signs of foolishness and learned how to guide our children toward wisdom.

Week 6: Work, Diligence, and Laziness - We studied the biblical view of work and how to instill a strong work ethic in our children.

THE LONG VIEW

Fatherhood is a marathon, not a sprint. There will be days when you feel like you're failing. Days when your children push back against everything you're trying to teach them. Days when you lose your temper, say the wrong thing, or miss an important moment.

But here's the truth: God doesn't expect you to be a perfect father. He just expects you to be a faithful one.

Keep showing up. Keep praying. Keep pointing your children to Jesus. Keep speaking words of life. Keep disciplining with love. Keep modeling integrity. Keep teaching wisdom. Keep working hard.

The seeds you're planting today may not bear fruit for years. But they will bear fruit. God's Word promises it: "Train up a child in the way he should go; even when he is old he will not depart from it" (Proverbs 22:6).

YOUR LEGACY

Every day, you're building a legacy. Not a legacy of perfection, but a legacy of faithfulness. A legacy of love. A legacy of pointing your children to something greater than themselves.

Years from now, your children may not remember every word you said or every lesson you taught. But they will remember how you made them feel. They will remember whether you were present. They will remember whether you loved them well. They will remember whether you pointed them to Jesus.

And if you do that—if you faithfully love them, guide them, and point them to Christ—you will have succeeded as a father.

MOVING FORWARD

As you move forward from this study, here are some final encouragements:

1. Stay in the Word. Don't let this be the end of your time in Proverbs. Keep reading, keep studying, keep learning. God's Word is living and active, and it has more to teach you. Dive deeper through daily journaling. You can try the *"Fathering Strong 30-Day Devotional and Journal"* available for sale on Amazon.

2. Stay connected to other fathers. You weren't meant to do this alone. Find other dads who are committed to raising their children in the fear of the Lord. Encourage each other, challenge each other, pray for each other.

3. Stay humble. You will make mistakes. You will fail. When you do, apologize to your children, ask for their forgiveness, and model what it looks like to depend on God's grace.

4. Stay focused on the gospel. Remember: you're not just trying to raise good kids. You're trying to raise children who know and love Jesus. Point them to the cross. Remind them of God's grace. Show them that their identity is in Christ, not in their performance.

5. Stay prayerful. Pray for your children every day. Pray for wisdom. Pray for patience. Pray for God to work in their hearts in ways you never could.

FINAL PRAYER

"Father, thank You for the privilege of being a dad. Thank You for entrusting these precious children to my care. I confess that I often feel inadequate for this task. But I know that You don't call the equipped—You equip the called.

Give me wisdom to lead my family well. Give me patience when I'm frustrated. Give me words of life when I'm tempted to speak harshly. Give me the courage to discipline with love. Give me integrity to model what I'm teaching. Give me discernment to guide my children away from foolishness and toward wisdom.

Most of all, help me to point my children to Jesus. May they see Him in me. May they know His love through my love. May they understand His grace through my grace. May they follow Him all the days of their lives.

I can't do this on my own, Lord. But with You, all things are possible. Thank You for Your faithfulness. Thank You for Your grace. Thank You for the gift of fatherhood.

In Jesus' name, Amen."

Dad, you've got this. Not because you're perfect, but because you serve a perfect God who loves your children even more than you do. Trust Him. Follow Him. And watch Him work in and through you to shape the next generation.

May God bless you and your family as you walk in wisdom together.

NOTES

38

The following section is for workshop facilitators using this content.

Thank you for your willingness to facilitate this six-week study through Proverbs. Leading other fathers on this journey is both a privilege and a responsibility. This guide will help you create an environment where men can grow, be challenged, and support one another in their calling as fathers.

YOUR ROLE AS FACILITATOR

You are not expected to be a perfect father or an expert teacher. Your role is to:

- **Create a safe space** where men can be honest about their struggles and failures
- **Guide the discussion** without dominating it
- **Model vulnerability** by sharing your own challenges and growth areas
- **Keep the group focused** on practical application, not just theoretical knowledge
- **Encourage accountability** among the participants
- **Point men to Scripture** as the ultimate authority
- **Pray for and with** the men in your group

Remember: you're a fellow traveler on this journey, not someone who has it all figured out. Your authenticity will give other men permission to be real.

PREPARING TO FACILITATE

BEFORE THE FIRST SESSION

- ➢ **Complete the study yourself first.** Work through all six weeks, filling out the worksheets and applying the principles to your own life. You can't lead where you haven't been.
- ➢ **Pray for each participant.** Ask God to prepare their hearts, reveal areas where they need to grow, and give them courage to change.
- ➢ **Prepare the logistics:**
    - o Secure a meeting location that's comfortable and private
    - o Decide on meeting time and duration (90-120 minutes recommended)
    - o Arrange for refreshments if possible (food helps men relax and connect)
    - o Make copies of worksheets or ensure participants have access to them
    - o Consider creating a group text or email chain for communication
- ➢ **Set clear expectations.** Prepare to communicate:
    - o The commitment required (six weeks, weekly attendance, daily worksheet work)
    - o The importance of confidentiality
    - o The value of vulnerability and honesty
    - o The expectation that men will actually do the work between sessions

BEFORE EACH SESSION

- ➢ **Review the week's material thoroughly.** Reread the chapter, review the key verses, and think through the discussion questions.

- ➢ **Pray specifically.** Ask God to guide the discussion, open hearts, and bring about real transformation.
- ➢ **Prepare your own story.** Think of a personal example from the week's topic that you can share to model vulnerability.
- ➢ **Arrive early.** Set up the space, have materials ready, and be available to greet men as they arrive.

WEEKLY SESSION FORMAT

Here's a suggested format for each 60-90 minute session:

OPENING (5-10 MINUTES)

- Welcome and brief check-in
- Opening prayer
- Quick review of last week's action steps (after Week 1)

TEACHING/DISCUSSION (30-40 MINUTES)

- Brief overview of the week's topic (5 minutes)
- Group discussion of key verses and principles (25-35 minutes)
- Personal application sharing

ACCOUNTABILITY AND APPLICATION (15-20 MINUTES)

- Review of Weekly Study Worksheet
- Sharing of specific action steps
- Pairing up for accountability

CLOSING (10 MINUTES)

- Prayer requests focused on fatherhood challenges
- Closing prayer
- Reminder of next week's reading

WEEK 1: THE FOUNDATION OF FATHERHOOD

Primary Goal: Establish the foundation that all wisdom begins with fearing the Lord. Help men see that they can't lead their children where they haven't been themselves.

Key Emphasis: This week is about personal relationship with God, not just religious activity. Challenge men to evaluate whether they're truly pursuing God or just going through the motions.

Opening Question: What brought you to this study? What do you hope to gain?

Key Discussion Questions:

1. What does "the fear of the LORD" mean to you? How have you seen this (or not seen this) modeled in your own life?
2. On a scale of 1-10, how would you rate your own pursuit of God? How do you think your children would rate it?
3. What are the biggest obstacles to modeling the fear of the Lord for your children?
4. Share one specific way you can demonstrate to your children this week that God is central to your life.
5. How does your relationship with your own father affect how you father your children?

Application Focus: Each man should identify one concrete way they will pursue God this week that their children can observe.

Watch For: Men who are new to faith or struggling in their relationship with God. Be prepared to offer additional support or resources.

Action Item: Make sure every man leaves with a clear plan for pursuing God this week that their children can observe.

WEEK 2: THE POWER OF YOUR WORDS

Primary Goal: Help men recognize the profound impact their words have on their children and commit to speaking life.

Key Emphasis: This isn't about being perfect—it's about being intentional. Even small changes in how we speak can have a huge impact.

Opening Question: Think back to your childhood. What's one thing your father said to you that you still remember today—for good or for bad?

Key Discussion Questions:

1. How would you describe the ratio of encouraging words to critical words you speak to each of your children?
2. Read Proverbs 18:21 together. How have you seen your words bring either "life" or "death" to your children?

3. What triggers you to speak harshly to your kids? What's really going on in your heart in those moments?
4. Which of your children needs to hear affirming words from you most right now? What's stopping you?
5. How comfortable are you with apologizing to your children when you've spoken harshly?

Application Focus: Each man should commit to writing a letter of affirmation to at least one child this week.

Facilitator Tip: This topic often brings up deep emotions and regret. Be prepared for men to share painful memories or recent failures. Create space for confession and grace.

Watch For: Deep regret and emotion. Many men carry guilt about harsh words they've spoken. Create space for confession and grace. Point them to the gospel.

Action Item: Make sure every man commits to writing a letter of affirmation to at least one child. Consider having them share excerpts (if they're comfortable) in the next session.

WEEK 3: DISCIPLINE AND LOVE

Primary Goal: Help men understand that biblical discipline flows from love and is aimed at the child's good, not the parent's convenience or anger.

Key Emphasis: Discipline and delight must go together. If children only experience correction and never affirmation, they'll grow up believing they can never please their father.

Opening Question: How were you disciplined as a child? How has that shaped your approach to disciplining your own children?

Key Discussion Questions:

1. What's the difference between discipline and punishment? Between discipline and abuse?
2. Read Proverbs 3:11-12. How does understanding God's discipline of us change how we discipline our children?
3. What's harder for you: being too harsh or being too lenient? Why?
4. How do you discipline when you're angry? What needs to change?
5. Do your children understand that you discipline them because you love them, or do they experience discipline as anger and rejection?
6. How do you balance discipline with delight? Do your children know you delight in them?

Application Focus: Each man should create a specific discipline plan for one recurring behavior issue with one of their children.

Facilitator Tip: This is often the most controversial topic. Some men come from backgrounds where discipline was harsh or abusive; others come from permissive backgrounds. Keep the focus on what Scripture says, not on cultural preferences or personal opinions.

Watch For: Strong emotions and disagreement. This topic can be triggering for men who were abused or who have abused their own children. Also watch for men who are too permissive and need to be challenged to actually discipline.

Action Item: Have each man create a specific, written discipline plan for one recurring behavior issue. This moves them from reactive to proactive.

Primary Goal: Help men see that character is caught more than taught, and that they must model integrity if they want their children to have it.

Key Emphasis: Integrity isn't about perfection—it's about consistency between who you are in public and who you are in private. It's also about owning your mistakes.

Opening Question: Who is someone you know who has real integrity? What makes them stand out?

Key Discussion Questions:

1. Read Proverbs 20:7. How does your integrity (or lack of it) affect your children?
2. In what areas are you tempted to compromise? How do you think your children perceive your integrity?
3. What "little white lies" do you tell that teach your children that honesty is optional?
4. How do you respond when your children catch you in a mistake or inconsistency?
5. What character qualities do you most want to see in your children? Are you modeling those qualities?
6. How do you teach character without being preachy or legalistic?

Application Focus: Each man should identify one area where they need to grow in integrity and share it with an accountability partner.

Facilitator Tip: Model vulnerability by sharing an area where you've compromised or struggled with integrity. This gives other men permission to be honest.

Watch For: Men who are living double lives or compromising in significant ways. Be prepared to have hard conversations privately.

Action Item: Challenge each man to identify one area where they need to grow in integrity and to share it with an accountability partner. This models the humility and honesty we want our children to have.

Primary Goal: Help men recognize the warning signs of foolishness in their children and equip them to guide their children toward wisdom.

Key Emphasis: We're all foolish sometimes. The question is whether we learn from our foolishness or persist in it. Help men distinguish between age-appropriate immaturity and dangerous rebellion.

Opening Question: What's the most foolish thing you did as a young person? What did you learn from it?

Key Discussion Questions:

1. Read Proverbs 12:15. How teachable are you? How do you respond when someone corrects you?
2. What warning signs of foolishness do you see in your children? How are you addressing them?
3. Which of the four types of fools (simple, stubborn, hardened, mocker) do you most worry about your children becoming? Why?
4. How do you help your children learn from their mistakes without rescuing them from consequences?
5. Who are your children's friends? How are those friendships influencing them?

6. How do you teach your children to be teachable?

Application Focus: Each man should have a specific conversation with their children about foolishness and wisdom this week.

Facilitator Tip: Help men distinguish between age-appropriate foolishness (immaturity) and dangerous foolishness (rebellion). Not every mistake is a crisis.

Watch For: Men who are dealing with rebellious teenagers or children who are making seriously foolish choices. These men may need additional support, resources, or referrals to counseling.

Action Item: Have each man identify one specific warning sign of foolishness in one of their children and create a plan to address it this week.

WEEK 6: WORK, DILIGENCE, AND LAZINESS

Primary Goal: Help men develop a biblical view of work and equip them to instill a strong work ethic in their children.

Key Emphasis: Work is a gift, not a curse. All honest work has dignity. We're teaching our children to work not just so they can be successful, but so they can serve God and others.

Opening Question: What did your father teach you about work? How has that shaped your work ethic?

Key Discussion Questions:

1. Read Proverbs 6:6-11. What does your work ethic teach your children about the value of work?
2. How do you balance working hard to provide for your family with being present with your family?
3. What responsibilities have you given your children? Are they age-appropriate? Are you holding them accountable?
4. Do your children see work as a burden or as a gift? How are you shaping their perspective?
5. What's the difference between teaching your children to work hard and teaching them that their worth comes from their performance?
6. How do you respond when your children want to quit something that's hard?

Application Focus: Each man should assign new age-appropriate responsibilities to their children and work alongside them on a project this week.

Facilitator Tip: Be sensitive to men who are unemployed or underemployed. This topic can bring up shame and discouragement. Emphasize that all honest work has dignity.

Watch For: Men who are workaholics and using work to avoid their families. Also watch for men who are unemployed or underemployed—this topic can bring up shame.

Action Item: Have each man assign new age-appropriate responsibilities to their children and commit to working alongside them on a project this week.

FACILITATING EFFECTIVE DISCUSSIONS

CREATING A SAFE ENVIRONMENT

- ➤ **Establish ground rules on the first night:**
  - ○ What's shared in the group stays in the group (confidentiality)
  - ○ No fixing, advising, or correcting unless asked
  - ○ Everyone participates, but no one dominates
  - ○ It's okay to pass if you're not ready to share
  - ○ Respect different parenting styles and family situations
  - ○ Focus on your own growth, not judging others
- ➤ **Model vulnerability.** Share your own struggles and failures first. This sets the tone and gives others permission to be real.
- ➤ **Protect the space.** If someone shares something deeply personal, thank them for their courage. If someone starts to dominate, gently redirect: "Thanks for sharing. Let's hear from someone else."
- ➤ **Avoid the "fix-it" trap.** Men naturally want to solve problems. Resist the urge to give advice unless asked. Sometimes men just need to be heard.

HANDLING DIFFICULT SITUATIONS

When someone dominates the discussion:

- "Thanks for that insight. Let's hear from someone who hasn't shared yet."
- Establish a "one share per question" rule if needed

When the group gets off-topic:

- "That's an interesting point, but let's come back to the question at hand."
- "We could talk about that for hours, but let's stay focused on [topic]."

When someone shares something concerning (abuse, addiction, severe marital problems):

- Thank them for their honesty
- Offer to talk with them privately after the session
- Connect them with appropriate resources (pastor, counselor, support group)
- Don't try to solve serious problems in the group setting

When there's awkward silence:

- Don't rush to fill it. Give men time to think.
- Rephrase the question if needed
- Share your own answer to get things started

When someone disagrees with the material:

- "That's an interesting perspective. What does Scripture say about this?"
- Keep bringing the discussion back to Proverbs and biblical principles
- Acknowledge that there's room for different applications of biblical principles

When someone is clearly not doing the work:

- Address it privately, not in the group
- Ask if there are obstacles you can help remove
- Remind them that they'll get out of this what they put into it
- If it continues, have a direct conversation about their commitment

USING THE WEEKLY STUDY WORKSHEET

The worksheet is the backbone of this study. It moves men from knowledge to action. Here's how to use it effectively:

DURING THE SESSION

➢ **Don't just ask "Did you do your worksheet?"** Instead, ask specific questions:
  - "What action steps did you commit to this week?"
  - "What did you actually do each day?"
  - "What wins did you have? What challenges?"
➢ **Have men share from their worksheets.** Go around the circle and have each man share:
  - One thing that stood out from the Scripture study
  - One specific action step they took
  - One thing they're grateful for about their children
➢ **Use the worksheet to create accountability.** Have men pair up and share their action steps for the coming week. Encourage them to check in with each other mid-week.

BETWEEN SESSIONS

➢ **Follow up.** Send a mid-week text or email reminding men to work on their worksheets and action steps.
➢ **Check in with strugglers.** If someone seems to be falling behind, reach out privately to encourage them.
➢ **Celebrate progress.** When you hear about a win, celebrate it publicly (with permission) in the next session.

BUILDING ACCOUNTABILITY

Accountability is crucial for lasting change. Here's how to build it into your group:

ACCOUNTABILITY PARTNERS

- Pair men up (or let them choose partners) in the first or second session
- Encourage them to exchange phone numbers and commit to weekly check-ins
- Provide specific questions for them to ask each other:
  - "Did you complete your action steps this week?"
  - "How did you speak to your children this week?"
  - "Where did you struggle?"
  - "How can I pray for you?"

GROUP ACCOUNTABILITY

- Start each session (after Week 1) with a brief check-in on last week's commitments
- Celebrate wins publicly
- Create a culture where it's safe to admit failure
- Remind men that accountability isn't about shame—it's about support

LONG-TERM ACCOUNTABILITY

- Encourage the group to continue meeting after the six weeks end
- Suggest they work through another resource together (like "Fathering Strong - A 90-day Devotional Journey")
- Help them establish ongoing rhythms of connection and accountability

PRAYER IN THE GROUP

Prayer should be central to your time together. Here's how to make it meaningful:

OPENING PRAYER

- Keep it brief (1-2 minutes)
- Ask God to open hearts, guide the discussion, and bring transformation
- Invite a different man to pray each week

CLOSING PRAYER

- Allow time for specific prayer requests related to fatherhood
- Write down requests so you can follow up
- Pray specifically for each man's children by name
- Consider having men pray in pairs or small groups if the group is large

BETWEEN SESSIONS

- Pray for each man and his family during the week
- Send encouraging texts letting men know you're praying for them
- Create a group prayer list that you update weekly

FINAL SESSION

- ➢ In your final session, take time to:

- ➢ **Celebrate growth.** Go around the circle and have each man share:
  - o One way they've grown as a father
  - o One specific change they've made
  - o One thing they're grateful for
- ➢ **Review key principles.** Briefly review the six topics and the main takeaway from each.
- ➢ **Look forward.** Discuss how the group will continue:
  - o Will you keep meeting?
  - o Will you work through another resource?
  - o How will you maintain accountability?
- ➢ **Pray together.** Have each man pray for the man on his right, specifically for his growth as a father.

CONTINUING THE JOURNEY

Consider these options for continuing after the six weeks:

- ➢ **Keep meeting monthly.** Continue gathering once a month for fellowship, accountability, and prayer.
- ➢ **Work through another resource.** Consider "Fathering Strong - A 90-day Devotional Journey" or another book on fatherhood.
- ➢ **Start a new group.** Have some of the men from your group facilitate new groups, multiplying the impact.
- ➢ **Create a dads' network.** Organize occasional events for fathers and children—service projects, camping trips, sports outings, etc.

RESOURCES FOR FACILITATORS

RECOMMENDED READING

- "Fathering Strong - God's Blueprint for Leading Your Family" by Bruce Stapleton
- "Fathering Strong: Fatherhood Awakening and 30-day Devotional and Journal" by Bruce Stapleton
- "Fathering Strong - A 90-day Devotional Journey" by Bruce Stapleton

ONLINE RESOURCES

- www.fatheringstrongbook.com/resources - Additional worksheets, discussion guides, and resources
- Download additional copies of the Weekly Study Worksheet
- Access video teachings and supplemental materials

WHEN TO REFER OUT

As a facilitator, you're not a professional counselor. Know when to refer men to additional help:

- **Abuse (past or present):** If a man discloses that he's abusing his children or was abused as a child, connect him with a pastor or professional counselor.
- **Addiction:** If a man is struggling with addiction (alcohol, drugs, pornography, etc.), connect him with a recovery program or counselor.
- **Severe marital problems:** If a man's marriage is in crisis, encourage him to seek marriage counseling.
- **Mental health issues:** If a man is dealing with depression, anxiety, or other mental health issues, encourage him to see a doctor or counselor.

Your role is to provide support and point men to appropriate resources, not to solve serious problems.

FINAL ENCOURAGEMENT

Leading this study is a significant investment of your time and energy. There will be moments when you wonder if it's making a difference. Trust that it is.

Every man who shows up is taking a courageous step. Every honest conversation is planting seeds. Every commitment to change is an act of faith. And God is at work in ways you can't see.

You're not just facilitating a Bible study—you're helping to shape the next generation. The impact of this study will ripple out through the lives of these men, their children, their grandchildren, and beyond.

Thank you for your faithfulness. May God bless you and give you wisdom as you lead.

"Let us not become weary in doing good, for at the proper time we will reap a harvest if we do not give up." (Galatians 6:9)

A Father's Heart

Weekly Study Worksheet

Week # _____ Topic _____ Date Started _____

Part 1: Personal Reflection

1. What challenges am I currently facing as a father?

2. What do I hope to learn or grow in this week?

3. On a scale of 1-10, how would I rate myself in this week's topic area? _____

Part 2: Scripture Study

Key Verse(s): Write out the main verse(s) for this week's study:

What stands out to me?

Part 3: Personal Application

Where I need to grow based on this week's study:

How this applies to each child:

Child: _____ Age/Stage:_____ How this applies: _____

Child: _____ Age/Stage:_____ How this applies: _____

Child: _____ Age/Stage:_____ How this applies: _____

Part 4: Action Steps

Three specific actions I'll take this week:

1. _____

2. _____

3. _____

Part 5: Prayer & Accountability

This week's prayer focus:

Scripture to memorize:

Accountability Partner: _____. Check-in Date: _____

Part 6: Daily Notes

Day	What I Did	Results/Lessons Learned
Mon		
Tues		
Wed		
Thu		
Fri		
Sat		
Sun		

Part 7: Weekly Review

Wins this week:

Challenges this week:

What God taught me:

Three things I'm grateful for about my children:

1. _____

2. _____

3. _____

"The fear of the LORD is the beginning of knowledge, but fools despise wisdom and instruction – Proverbs 1:7

www.ingramcontent.com/pod-product-compliance
Lightning Source LLC
Chambersburg PA
CBHW080904120626
46555CB00008B/2955